THE
ABCs
OF
DEMOCRACY

TO MY PARENTS, FOR NURTURING ME;
MY FAMILY, FOR STRENGTHENING ME;
AND MY COMMUNITY, FOR SUPPORTING ME
—HSJ

Grand Central Publishing
Hachette Book Group
1290 Avenue of the Americas, New York, NY 10104
grandcentralpublishing.com
@grandcentralpub

First Edition: November 2024

Grand Central Publishing is a division of Hachette Book Group, Inc. The Grand Central Publishing name and logo is a registered trademark of Hachette Book Group, Inc.

The publisher is not responsible for websites (or their content) that are not owned by the publisher.

The Hachette Speakers Bureau provides a wide range of authors for speaking events. To find out more, go to hachettespeakersbureau.com or email HachetteSpeakers@hbgusa.com.

Grand Central Publishing books may be purchased in bulk for business, educational, or promotional use. For information, please contact your local bookseller or the Hachette Book Group Special Markets Department at special.markets@hbgusa.com.

ISBN: 978-1-5387-7036-8

Printed in the United States of America

PHX

1   3   5   7   9   10   8   6   4   2

THE
ABCs
OF
DEMOCRACY

BY **HAKEEM JEFFRIES**

ILLUSTRATED BY **SHANIYA CARRINGTON**

INTRODUCTION

ON THE LAST DAY of November 2022, House Democrats
gathered on Capitol Hill to elevate a new leadership team during
a fragile moment in our nation's history. Earlier that month, we
had narrowly lost control of the House of Representatives after
dramatically overperforming expectations. Shortly thereafter,
Speaker Nancy Pelosi announced that she was stepping down
from leadership after a legendary twenty years at the helm.
The responsibility would fall to a new generation of public
servants to lead House Democrats into the future.

I had the honor of being unanimously elected by my
colleagues as the incoming House Minority Leader, ninety-
eight years to the day the late great Shirley Chisholm—my
Congresswoman—was born in Brooklyn. Only in America. The
new Congress began in early January, approximately two years
after a former President had incited a violent mob to attack the
Capitol, part of a disgraceful effort to halt the peaceful transfer
of power. As Minority Leader, I would be the first member to
address the entire body before handing over the gavel to the
incoming Speaker of the House.

Our country is in the midst of an identity crisis, with many
turning their backs on the traditional values and institutions

that have made the United States the greatest democracy in the history of the world. Nearly 250 years strong, we have overcome countless challenges, including slavery, the Civil War, Jim Crow, the Great Depression, and two World Wars. Yet new obstacles have emerged as part of our enduring march toward a more perfect union.

Unquestionably, we have a powerful military that will continue to serve as an arsenal for democracy as once envisioned by President Franklin Delano Roosevelt. But military might alone is insufficient. We are not free simply because we are strong. We are strong because we are free. That freedom, and the very strength that flows from it, is now at risk.

America is at a fork in the road. Which direction will we choose?

Against this backdrop of uncertainty, I appeared before the House of Representatives at 12:57 a.m. on Saturday, January 7, 2023, the first African-American in history to ever hold this position. Humbly standing on the shoulders of giants like Barbara Jordan and John Lewis, I delivered the opening speech of the 118th Congress. In that moment, there was an urgent need to speak with clarity about the existential stakes facing the nation.

America can follow the path of enlightenment or succumb to the forces that galvanize the ugly underbelly of any society. What better way to present the critical choice our country confronts, I concluded, than to view it through the elegant lens of the alphabet.

This book animates my remarks and uses the power of illustration to provide a blueprint for a brighter day.

America is indeed a resilient nation.

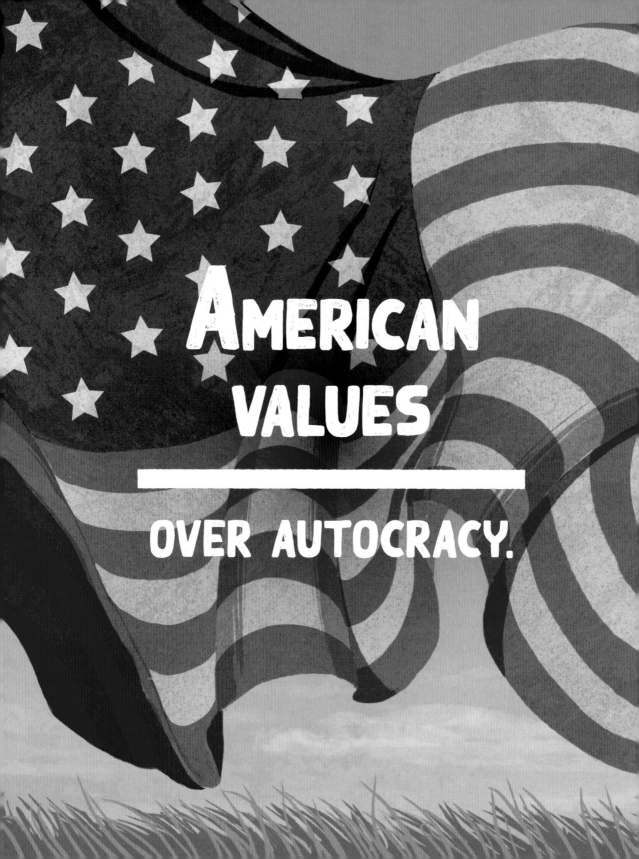

AMERICAN VALUES

OVER AUTOCRACY.

BENEVOLENCE

OVER BIGOTRY.

THE CONSTITUTION

OVER THE CULT.

ECONOMIC OPPORTUNITY

OVER EXTREMISM.

GOVERNING

OVER GASLIGHTING.

HOPEFULNESS

OVER HATRED.

INCLUSION

OVER ISOLATION.

E PLURIBUS UNUM

JUSTICE

OVER JUDICIAL OVERREACH.

KNOWLEDGE

OVER KANGAROO COURTS.

LIBERTY

OVER LIMITATION.

MATURITY

OVER MAR-A-LAGO.

NORMALCY

OVER NEGATIVITY.

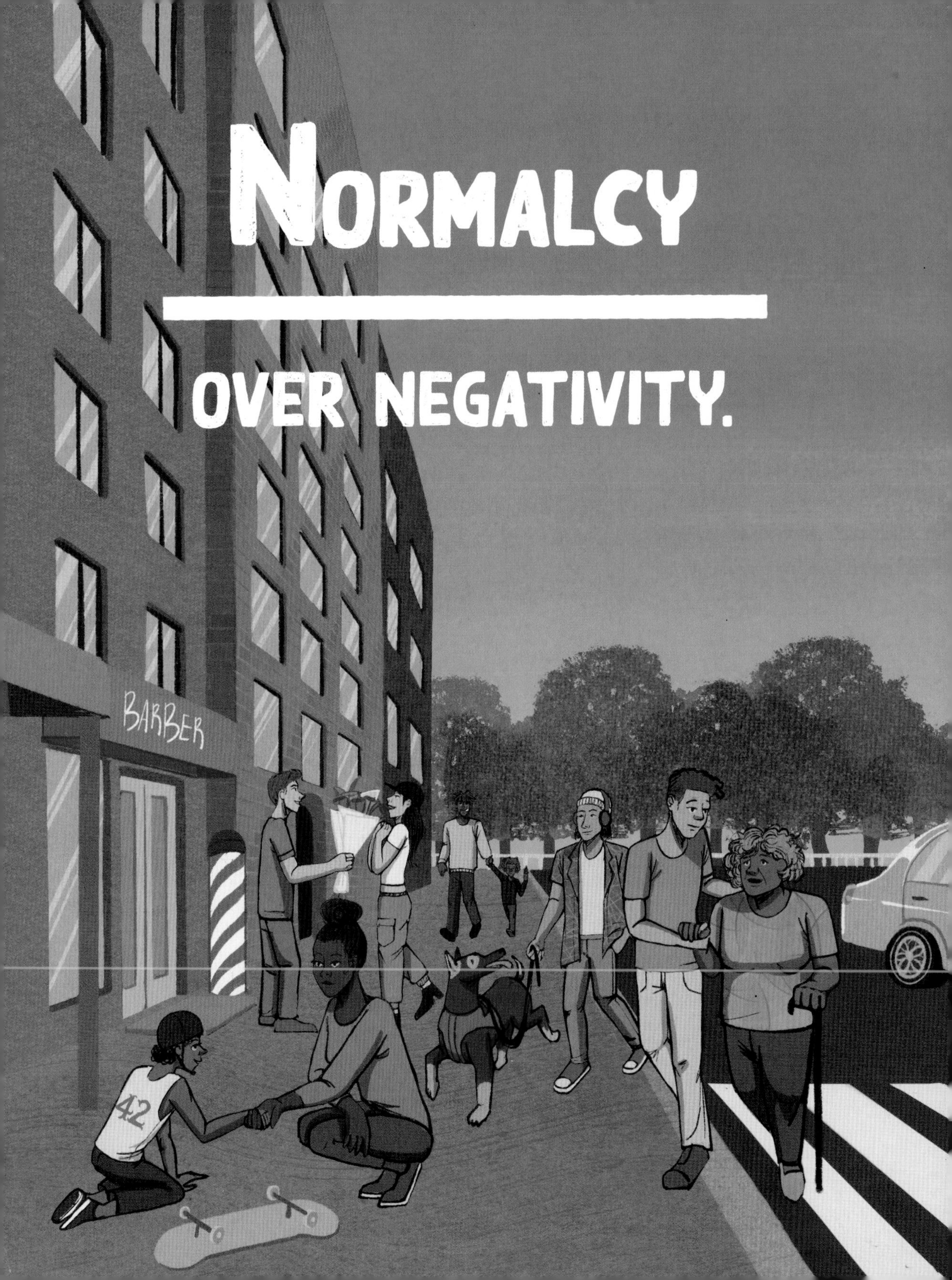

Substance

OVER SLANDER.

TRIUMPH

OVER TYRANNY.

UNDERSTANDING

OVER UGLINESS.

VOTING RIGHTS

OVER VOTER SUPPRESSION.

Xenial

OVER XENOPHOBIA.

YES WE CAN

OVER YOU CAN'T DO IT.

AND ZEALOUS REPRESENTATION

OVER ZERO-SUM CONFRONTATION.